Occult Arts

By William Q. Judge

Copyright © 2021 Lamp of Trismegistus. All rights reserved. No part of this publication may be reproduced or transmitted in any form or by any means, electronic or mechanical, including photocopying, recording, or by any information storage and retrieval system, without permission in writing from Lamp of Trismegistus. Reviewers may quote brief passages.

ISBN: 978-1-63118-559-5

Esoteric Classics

Other Books in this Series and Related Titles

Aurora of the Philosophers by Paracelsus (978-1-63118-507-6)

Clairvoyance and Psychic Abilities by A Besant &c (978-1-63118-403-1)

The Feminine Occult by various authors (978-1-63118-711-7)

Rosicrucian Rules, Secret Signs, Codes and Symbols by various (978-1-63118-488-8)

An Outline of Theosophy by C W Leadbeater (978-1-63118-452-9)

Paracelsus, the Four Elements and Their Spirits by M P Hall (978-1-63118-400-0)

The Stone of the Philosophers by A E Waite (978-1-63118-509-0)

Essays on the Esoteric Tradition of Karma by A Besant &c (978-1-63118-426-0)

The Use of Evil by Annie Besant (978-1-63118-532-8)

The Alchemical Catechism of Paracelsus by Paracelsus (978-1-63118-513-7)

Alchemy in the Nineteenth Century by Helena P Blavatsky (978-1-63118-446-8)

Qabbalistic Teachings and the Tree of Life by M P Hall (978-1-63118-482-6)

The Devil in Love by Jacques Cazotte (978–1–63118–499–4)

Fortune-Telling with Dice by Astra Cielo (978-1-63118-466-6)

History, Analysis and Secret Tradition of the Tarot by Hall &c (978-1-63118-445-1)

Crystal Vision Through Crystal Gazing by Frater Achad (978-1-63118-455-0)

The Golden Verses of Pythagoras: Five Translations (978-1-63118-479-6)

Arcane Formulas or Mental Alchemy by W W Atkinson (978-1-63118-459-8)

The Machinery of the Mind by Dion Fortune (978-1-63118-451-2)

The A E Waite Reader: A Selection of Occult Essays (978-1-63118-515-1)

The Leadbeater Reader: A Selection of Occult Essays (978-1-63118-483-3)

Audio versions are also available on Audible, Amazon and Apple

Other Books in this Series and Related Titles

On the Cave of the Nymphs in the Odyssey by Thomas Taylor (978-1-63118-505-2)

Occult Symbolism of Animals, Insects, Reptiles, Fish & Birds (978-1-63118-420-8)

The Poem of Hashish by A Crowley & C Baudelaire (978-1-63118-484-0)

Brothers & Builders by Joseph Fort Newton (978-1-63118-506-9)

The Kabbalah of Masonry & Related Writings by E Levi &c (978-1-63118-453-6)

A Collection of Fiction and Essays by Occult Writers on Supernatural and Metaphysical Subjects by various (978–1–63118–510–6)

The Sepher Yetzirah and the Qabalah by M P Hall (978-1-63118-481-9)

Cloud Upon the Sanctuary by Waite & K Eckartshausen (978-1-63118-438-3)

The Hymns of Hermes by G R S Mead (978-1-63118-405-5)

The Secrets of Enoch by Enoch (978-1-63118-449-9)

The Hidden Mysteries of Christianity by Annie Besant (978–1–63118–534–2)

The Sword of Welleran and Other Stories by Lord Dunsany (978-1-63118-501-4)

The Eleusinian Mysteries and Rites by Dudley Wright (978–1–63118–530–4)

Gnosis of the Mind by G. R. S. Mead (978-1-63118-408-6)

The First and Second Gospels of the Infancy of Jesus Christ (978-1-63118-415-4)

The Life of Pythagoras by Porphyry (978-1-63118-512-0)

Essays on Ancient Magic by H. P. Blavatsky (978-1-63118-535-9)

Rosicrucians and Speculative Masonry in the Seventeenth Century (978-1-63118-489-5)

The Influence of Pythagoras on Freemasonry and Other Essays (978-1-63118-404-8)

The Path of Light: A Manual of Maha-Yana Buddhism (978-1-63118-471-0)

Tao Te Ching & Commentary by Lao Tzu & C Johnston (978-1-63118-495-6)

Audio versions are also available on Audible, Amazon and Apple

Table of Contents

Introduction...7

Occult Arts

Precipitation...9

Disintegration – Reintegration...23

Some Propositions by Madame Blavatsky...31

INTRODUCTION

The word "esoteric" can be difficult to define. Esotericism in general can be seen less as a system of beliefs and more as a category, which encompasses numerous, different systems of beliefs. It's a bit of juxtaposition, since the word "esoteric" indicates something that few people know about, while the term itself broadly covers numerous philosophies, practices, areas of study and belief systems.

In a greater sense, Esotericism acts as a storehouse for secret knowledge, which is often considered ancient (by *tradition, if not by fact),* passed down from generation to generation, in private. At various times in history, simply possessing the knowledge of some of these subjects, was considered illegal and a jailable offence, if discovered. This usually included such general topics as Alchemy, Pharmacology, Qabalah, Hermeticism, Occultism, Ceremonial Magic, Astrology, Divination, Rosicrucianism and so on. Collectively, these areas of study were often referred to as the esoteric sciences.

Sometimes, the outer garment of a subject isn't esoteric, while what is hidden beneath it, is. As an example, Freemasonry isn't necessarily esoteric by nature (at *least not anymore),* but certain signs, passwords and handshakes given to the candidate during their initiation, are in fact, esoteric, in the sense that they are hidden from the general public.

Today, in the twenty-first century, such topics are readily available at bookstores across the country, and numerous mainsteam publishers offer beginners guides and coffee-table volumes on many of these subjects, intended for mass appeal. Books like *"The Secret"* have turned previously arcane topics into household knowledge. All that being the case, however, it isn't to say that there still aren't buried secrets to uncover, ancient wisdom being ignored and forgotten mysteries to be explored. In fact, it is often that we are only able to further our own studies by standing on the shoulders of these disappearing giants.

Lamp of Trismegistus is doing its part to help preserve humanity's esoteric history by making some of these classics available to those students who are seeking to unearth the knowledge of these ancient colossi.

So, be sure to check other titles from our *Esoteric Classics* series, as well as our *Occult Fiction*, *Theosophical Classics*, *Foundations of Freemasonry Series*, *Supernatural Fiction*, *Paranormal Research Series*, *Studies in Buddhism* and our *Christian Apocrypha Series*. You can also download the audio versions of most of these titles from Amazon, Apple or Audible, for learning on the go.

OCCULT ARTS

PRECIPITATION

The word "precipitation" means to throw upon or within. This term is used in chemistry to describe the fact of a substance, held or suspended in fluid, being made to disengage itself from the intimate union with the fluid and to fall upon the bottom of the receptacle in which it is held; in the use of applied electricity it may be used to describe the throwing upon a metal or other plate, of particles of another metal held in suspension in the fluid of the electric bath. These two things are done every day in nearly all the cities of the world, and are so common as to be ordinary. In photography the same effect is described by the word "develop", which is the appearing on the surface of the sensitized gelatin plate of the image caught by the camera. In chemical precipitation the atoms fall together and become visible as a separate substance in the fluid; in photography the image made by an alteration of the atoms composing the whole surface appears in the mass of the sensitized plate.

In both cases we have the coming forth into visibility of that which before was invisible. In the case of precipitation of a substance in the form of a powder at the bottom of the receptacle containing the fluid, there is distinctly, (*a*) before the operation an invisibility of a mass of powder, (*b*) upon applying the simple means for precipitation the sudden coming into sight of that which was before unseen.

And precisely as the powder may be precipitated in the fluid, so also from the air there can be drawn and precipitated the various metals and substances suspended therein. This has been so often done by chemists and others that no proofs are needed.

The ancients and all the occultists of past and present have always asserted that all metals, substances, pigments, and materials exist in the air held in suspension, and this has been admitted by modern science. Gold, silver, iron and other metals may be volatilized by heat so as to float unseen in the air, and this is also brought about every day in various mines and factories of the world. It may therefore be regarded as established beyond controversy that as a physical fact precipitation of substances, whether as merely carbon or metal, is possible and is done every day. We can then take another step with the subject.

Is it possible to precipitate by will-power and use of occult laws upon a surface of wood, paper, metal, stone, or glass a mass of substance in lines or letters or other combinations so as to produce an intelligible picture or a legible message? For modern science this is not possible yet; for the Adept it is possible, has been done, and will be still performed. It has also been done unintelligently and as mere passive agents or channels, among mediums in the ranks of European and American spiritualists. But in this latter case it has the value, and no more than that, of the operations of nature upon and with natural objects, to be imitated by conscious and intelligently-acting man when he has learned how, by what means, and when. The medium is only a passive controlled agent or channel who is ignorant of the laws and forces employed, as well as not knowing what is the intelligence at work, nor whether that intelligence is outside or a part of the medium.

The Adept, on the other hand, knows how such a precipitation can be done, what materials may be used, where those materials are obtainable, how they can be drawn out of the air, and what general and special laws must be taken into account. That this operation can be performed I know of my own knowledge; I have seen it done, watching the process as it proceeded, and have seen the effect produced without a failure. One of these instances I will give later on.

Precipitation of words or messages from Adepts has been much spoken of in the Theosophical Society's work, and the generality of persons have come to some wrong conclusions as to what they must be like, as well as how they are done and what materials may be and are used. Most suppose as follows:

1. That the precipitated messages are on rice paper;

2. That they are invariably in one or two colors of some sort of chalk or carbon;

3. That in every case they are incorporated into the fiber of the paper so as to be ineradicable;

4. That in each case when finished they came from Tibet or some other distant place invisibly through the air.

5. That all of them are done by the hand of the Adept and are in his handwriting as commonly used by him or them.

While it is true in fact that each of the above particulars may have been present in some of the cases and that every one of the above is possible, it is not correct that the above are right as settled facts and conclusions. For the way, means, methods, conditions, and results of precipitation are as varied and numerous as any other operation of nature. The following is laid down by some of the masters of this art as proper to be kept in mind.

(*a*), A precipitated picture or message may be on any sort of paper.

(*b*), It may be in black or any other pigment.

(*c*), It may be in carbon, chalk, ink, paint, or other fluid or substance.

(*d*), It may be on any sort of surface or any kind of material.

(*e*), It may be incorporated in the fiber of the paper and be thus ineffaceable, or lie upon the surface and be easily eradicated.

(*f*), It may come through the air as a finished message on paper or otherwise, or it may be precipitated at once at the place of reception on any kind of substance and in any sort of place.

(*g*), It is not necessarily in the handwriting of the Adept, and may be in the hand comprehended by the recipient and a language foreign to the Adept, or it may be in the actual hand of the Adept, or lastly in a cipher known to a few and not decipherable by any one without its key.

(*h*), As matter of fact the majority of the messages precipitated or sent by the Adepts in the history of the Theosophical Society have been in certain forms of English writing not the usual writing of those Adepts, but adopted for use in the Theosophical movement because of a fore-knowledge that the principal language of that movement would for some time be the English.

Some messages have been written and precipitated in Hindi or Urdu, some in Hindustani, and some in a cipher perfectly unintelligible to all but a few persons. These assertions I make upon personal knowledge founded on observation, on confirmation through an inspection of messages, and on logical deduction made from facts and philosophical propositions. In the first place, the Adepts referred to — and not including silent ones of European birth — are Asiatics whose languages are two different Indian ones: hence their usual handwriting is not English and not Roman in the letters. *Secondly*, it is a fact long suspected and to many well known both in and out of the Theosophical Society that the Fraternity of Adepts has a cipher which they employ for many of their communications: that, being universal, is not their handwriting. *Thirdly*, in order to send any one a precipitated message in English it is not necessary for the Adept to know that language; if you know it, that is enough; for, putting the thought in your brain, he sees it there as your language in your brain, and using that model causes the message to appear. But if he is acquainted with the language you use, it is all the easier for the Adept to give you the message exactly as he forms it in his brain at first. The same law applies to all cases of precipitation by an alleged spirit through a medium who does not know at all how it is done: in such a case it is all done by natural and chiefly irresponsible agents who can only imitate what is in the brains concerned in the matter.

These points being considered, the questions remain, How is it all done, what is the process, what are the standards of judgment, of criticism, and of proof to the outer sense, is imposition possible, and, if so, how may it be prevented?

As to the last, the element of faith or confidence can never be omitted until one has gotten to a stage where within oneself the true standard and power of judging are developed. Just as forgery may be done on this physical plane, so also may it be done on the other and unseen planes and its results shown on this. Ill-disposed souls may work spiritual wickedness, and ignorant living persons may furnish idle, insincere, and lying models for not only ill-disposed souls that are out of the body, but also for mere sprites that are forces in nature of considerable power but devoid of conscience and mind. Mind is not needed in them, for they use the mind of man, and merely with this aid work the hidden laws of matter. But this furnishes some protection illustrated in the history of spiritualism, where so many messages are received that on their face are nonsense and evidently but the work of elementals who simply copy what the medium or the sitter is vainly holding in mind. In those cases some good things have come, but they are never beyond the best thought of the persons who, living, thus attempt to speak with the dead.

Any form of writing once written on earth is imprinted in the astral light and remains there as a model. And if it has been used much, it is all the more deeply imprinted. Hence the fact that H. P. Blavatsky, who once was the means for messages coming from the living Adepts, is dead and gone is not a reason why the same writing should not be used again. It was used so much in letters to Mr. Sinnett from which *Esoteric Buddhism* was written and in many other letters from the same source that its model or matrix is deeply cut in the astral light. For it would be folly and waste of time for the Adepts to make new models every time any one died. They would naturally use the old model. There is no special sanctity in the particular model used by them, and any good clairvoyant can find that matrix in the astral light. Hence from this, if true, two things follow:

>(*a*), that new communications need not be in a new style of writing, and

>(*b*), there is a danger that persons who seek either clairvoyants or mesmerized *lucides* may be imposed on and made to think they have messages from the Adepts, when in fact they have only imitations.

The safeguard therein is that, if these new messages are not in concordance with old ones known to be from their first appointed channel, they are not genuine in their source, however phenomenally made. Of course for the person who has the power inside to see for himself, the safeguard is different and more certain. This position accords with occult philosophy, it has been stated by the Adepts themselves, it is supported by the facts of psychic investigation inside the ranks of Spiritualism, of Theosophy, of human life.

It is well known that mediums have precipitated messages on slates, on paper, and on even the human skin, which in form and manner exactly copied the hand of one dead and gone, and also of the living. The model for the writing was in the aura of the enquirer, as most mediums are not trained enough to be able independently to seek out and copy astral models not connected with some one present. I exclude all cases where the physical or astral hand of the medium wrote the message, for the first is fraud and the second a psychological trick. In the last case, the medium gazing into the astral light sees the copy or model there and merely makes a *facsimile* of what is thus seen, but which is invisible to the sitter. There is no exemption from law in favor of the Adepts, and the images they make or cause to be made in astral ether remain as the property of the race; indeed in their case, as they have a sharp and vivid power of engraving, so to say, in the astral light, all the images made there by them are deeper and more lasting than those cut by the ordinary and weak thoughts and acts of our undeveloped humanity.

The best rule for those who happen to think they are in communication with Adepts through written messages is to avoid those that contradict what the Adepts have said before; that give the lie to their system of philosophy; that, as has happened, pretend that H. P. B. was mistaken in her life for what she said and is now sorry. All such, whether done with intention or without it, are merely *bombinans in vacuo*, sound that has no significance, a confusion between words and knowledge delusive and vain altogether. And as we know that the Adepts have written that they have no concern with the progress of selfish science, it must be true that messages which go on merely to the end of establishing some scientific proposition or that are not for the furtherance especially of Brotherhood cannot be from them, but are the product of other minds, a mere extension through occult natural law of theories of weak men. This leads to the proposition that:

> Precipitation of a message is not *per se* evidence that it is from one of our White Adepts of the Great Lodge.

The outer senses cannot give a safe final judgment upon a precipitated message, they can only settle such physical questions as how it came, through whom, the credibility of the person, and whether any deception on the objective plane has been practiced. The inner senses, including the great combining faculty or power of intuition, are the final judges. The outer have to do solely with the phenomenal part, the inner deal with the causes and the real actors and powers.

As precipitations have been phenomenally made through "controlled" mediums who are themselves ignorant of the laws and forces at work, these are but strange phenomena proving the existence of a power in Nature either related to human mind or wholly unrelated to it. These are not the exercise of Occult Arts, but simply the operation of natural law, however recondite and obscure. They are like the burning of a flame, the falling of water, or the rush of the lightning, whereas when the Adept causes a flame to appear where there is no wick, or a sound to come where there is no vibrating visible surface, occult art is using the same laws and forces which with the medium are automatically and unconsciously operated by subtle parts of the medium's nature and "nature spirits", as well as what we know as *kama-lokic* human entities, in combination. And here the outer senses deal solely with the outer phenomena, being unable to touch in the least on the unseen workings behind. So they can only decide whether a physical fraud has been practiced; they can note the day, the hour, the surrounding circumstances, but no more.

But if one hitherto supposed to be in communication with the White Adepts comes to us and says "Here is a message from one of Those", then if we have not independent power in ourselves of deciding the question on inner knowledge, the next step is either to believe the report or disbelieve it. In the case of H.P. B., in whose presence and through whom messages were said to come from the White Adepts, it was all the time, at the final analysis, a matter of faith in those who confessedly had and have no independent personal power to know by the use of their own inner senses. But there intuition, one of the inner powers, decided for the genuineness of the report and the authentication of the messages. She herself put it tersely in this way: "If you think no Mahatma wrote the theories I have given of man and nature and if you do not believe my report, then you have to conclude that I did it all." The latter conclusion would lead to the position that her acts, phenomena, and writings put her in the position usually accorded by us to a Mahatma. As to the letters or messages of a personal nature, each one had and has to decide for himself whether or not to follow the advice given.

Another class of cases is where a message is found in a closed letter, on the margin or elsewhere on the sheet. The outer senses decide whether the writer of the letter inserted the supposed message or had some one else do it, and that must be decided on what is known of the character of the person. If you decide that the correspondent did not write it nor have anyone else do so, but that it was injected phenomenally, then the inner senses must be used. If they are untrained, certainly the matter becomes one of faith entirely, unless intuition is strong enough to decide correctly that a wise as well as powerful person caused the writing to appear there. Many such messages have been received in the history of the T. S. Some came in one way, some in another; one might be in a letter from a member of the Society, another in a letter from an outsider wholly ignorant of these matters. In every case, unless the recipient had independent powers developed within, no judgment on mere outer phenomena would be safe.

It is very difficult to find cases such as the above, because *first*, they are extremely rare, and *second*, the persons involved do not wish to relate them, since the matter transmitted had a purely personal bearing. A fancy may exist that in America or England or London such messages, generally considered bogus by enemies and outsiders, are being constantly sent and received, and that persons in various quarters are influenced to this or that course of action by them, but this is pure fancy, without basis in fact so far as the knowledge and experience of the writer extend. While precipitations phenomenally by the use of occult power and in a way unknown to science are possible and have occurred, that is not the means employed by the White Adepts in communicating with those thus favored. They have disciples with whom communication is already established and carried on, most generally through the inner ear and eye, but sometimes through the prosaic mail. In these cases no one else is involved and no one else has the right to put questions. The disciple reserves his communications for the guidance of his own action, unless he or she is directed to tell another. To spread broadcast a mass of written communications among those who are willing to accept them without knowing how to judge would be the sheerest folly, only productive of superstition and blind credulity. This is not the aim of the Adepts nor the method they pursue. And this digression will be excused, it being necessary because the subject of precipitation as a fact has been brought up very prominently. I may further digress to say that no amount of precipitations, however clear of doubt and fraud as to time, place, and outward method, would have the slightest effect on my mind or action unless my own intuition and inner senses confirmed them and showed them to be from a source which, should call for my attention and concurrence.

How, then, is this precipitation done, and what is the process? This question brings up the whole of the philosophy offered in the Secret Doctrine. For if the postulate of the metaphysical character of the Cosmos is denied, if the supreme power of the disciplined mind is not admitted, if the actual existence of an inner and real world is negated, if the necessity and power of the image-making faculty are disallowed, then such precipitation is an impossibility, always was, and always will be. Power over mind, matter, space, and time depends on several things and positions. Needed for this are: Imagination raised to its highest limit, desire combined with will that wavers not, and a knowledge of the occult chemistry of Nature. All must be present or there will be no result.

Imagination is the power to make in the ether an image. This faculty is limited by any want of the training of mind and increased by good mental development. In ordinary persons imagination is only a vain and fleeting fancy, which makes but a small impression comparatively in the ether. This power, when well-trained, makes a matrix in ether wherein each line, word, letter, sentence, color, or other mark is firmly and definitely made. Will, well-trained, must then be used to draw from the ether the matter to be deposited, and then, according to the laws of such an operation, the depositing matter collects in masses within the limits of the matrix and becomes from its accumulation visible on the surface selected. The will, still at work, has then to cut off the mass of matter from its attraction to that from whence it came. This is the whole operation, and who then is the wiser? Those learned in the schools laugh, and well they may, for there is not in science anything to correspond, and many of the positions laid down are contrary to several received opinions. But in Nature there are vast numbers of natural effects produced by ways wholly unknown to science, and Nature does not mind the laughter, nor should any disciple.

But how is it possible to inject such a precipitation into a closed letter? The ether is all-pervading, and the envelope or any other material bar is no bar to it. In it is carried the matter to be deposited, and as the whole operation is done on the other side of visible nature up to the actual appearance of the deposit, physical obstructions do not make the slightest difference.

It is necessary to return for a moment to the case of precipitations through mediums. Here the matrix needs no trained imagination to make it, nor trained will to hold it. In the astral light the impressions are cut and remain immovable; these are used by the elementals and other forces at work, and no disturbing will of sitter being able to interfere — simply from blind ignorance — there is no disturbance of the automatic unconscious work. In the sitter's aura are thousands of impressions, which remain unmoved because all attention has been long ago withdrawn. And the older or simpler they are the more firmly do they exist. These constitute also a matrix through which the nature spirits work.

I can properly finish this with the incident mentioned at the beginning. It was with H.P. B. I was sitting in her room beside her, the distance between us being some four feet. In my hand I held a book she never had had in her possession and that I had just taken from the mail. It was clear of all marks, its title page was fresh and clean, no one had touched it since it left the bookseller. I examined its pages and began to read. In about five minutes a very powerful current of what felt like electricity ran up and down my side on the skin, and I looked up at her. She was looking at me and said "What do you read?" I had forgotten the title, as it was one I had never seen before, and so I turned back to the title page. There at the top on the margin where it had not been before was a sentence of two lines of writing in ink, and the ink was wet, and the writing was that of H.P. B. who sat before me. She had not touched the book, but by her knowledge of occult law, occult chemistry, and occult will, she had projected out of the ink-bottle before her the ink to make the sentence, and of course it was in her own handwriting, as that was the easiest way to do it. Hence my own physical system was used to do the work, and the instant of its doing was when I felt the shock on the skin. This is to be explained in the way I have outlined, or it is to be all brushed aside as a lie or as a delusion of mine. But those last I can not accept, for I know to the contrary, and further I know that the advice, for such it was, in that sentence was good. I followed it, and the result was good. Several other times also have I seen her precipitate on different surfaces, and she always said it was no proof of anything whatever save the power to do the thing, admitting that black and white magicians could do the same thing, and saying that the only safety for any one in the range of such forces was to be pure in motive, in thought, and in act.

DISINTEGRATION — REINTEGRATION

Just as we have seen that precipitation is known to material science in electroplating and other arts, so also is it true that in most departments of applied science disintegration is understood, and that here and there reintegration of such substances as diamonds has been successfully accomplished. But these are all by mechanical or chemical processes. The question here is, whether — as in respect to precipitation — the occult powers of man and nature can bring about the results. Has any one ever reduced a solid object to impalpable powder and then at a distant place restored the object to its former state? And, if so, how is it done? As to the first, I can only say that I have seen this done, and that many testimonies have been offered by others at various times for the same thing. In the records of Spiritualism there are a great many witnesses to this effect, and accepting all cases in that field which are free from fraud the same remarks as were made about precipitation apply. With mediums it is unconsciously done; the laws governing the entire thing are unexplained by the medium or the alleged spirits; the whole matter is involved in obscurity so far as that cult is concerned, and certainly the returning spooks will give no answer until they find it in the brain of some living person. But the fact remains that among powerful physical mediums the operation has been performed by some unknown force acting under hidden guidance, itself as obscure.

This feat is not the same as apportation, the carrying or projecting of an object through space, whether it be a human form or any other thing. Buddhist and Hindu stories alike teem with such apportations; it is alleged of Apollonius the Greek, of Tyana; Christian saints are said to have been levitated and carried. In the Buddhist stories many of the immediate disciples of Buddha, both during his life and after his death, are said to have flown through the air from place to place; and in the history of Rama, some ascetics and Hanuman an the monkey god are credited with having so levitated themselves.

So many metals and minerals may be volatilized that we may take it as a general rule that all — until an exception is met with — are volatile under the proper conditions. Gold is slow in this respect, some observers having kept it heated for two months with no loss of weight, and others found a small loss after exposing it to violent heat; a charge of electricity will dissipate it. Silver volatilizes at red heat, and iron can also be similarly affected. But when we come to wood or softer vegetable matter, the separation of its atoms from each other is more easily accomplished. The process of disintegrating by the use of occult forces and powers is akin to what we can do on the material plane. The result is the same, however the means employed may vary; that is, the molecules are pressed apart from each other and kept so. If by mechanical, chemical, and electrical processes man can bring about this result, there is no reason, save in an asserted unproved denial, why it may not be done by the use of the mind and will. Rarity or unusualness proves nothing; when the telegraph was new its rarity proved nothing against its actuality; and it is every day becoming more the fashion to admit than it is to deny the possibility of anything in the realm opened up by our knowledge of electricity, while the probability is left merely to suspended judgment.

Passing from material science to the medical researches into hypnotism, we find there the stepping-stone between the purely mechanical physical processes and the higher subtler realm of the mind, the will, and the imagination. Here we see that the powerful forces wielded by the mind are able to bring about effects on bone, flesh, blood, and skin equal in measure to many processes of disintegration or volatilization. But in every-day life we have similar suggestive facts. In the blush and the cold chill, which come instantaneously over the whole frame, spreading in a second from the mental source, are effects upon matter made directly from mind. Even a recollection of an event can easily bring on this physical effect. In hypnotic experiments the skin, blood, and serum may be altered so as to bring out all the marks and changes of a burn or abrasion. In these cases the mind influenced by another mind makes an image through which the forces act to cause the changes. It is possible because, as so often asserted by the ancient sages, the Universe is really Will and Idea, or, as is so well put in a letter from one of the Adepts, "*the machinery of the cosmos is not only occult, it is ideal: and the higher metaphysics must be understood if one is to escape from the illusions under which men labor and which will continually lead them into the adoption of false systems respecting life and nature in consequence of the great 'collective hallucination' in which modern scientific persons glory so much, but which they do not call by that name.*"

So much, then, being briefly premised, it is said by the schools of occultism, known not only since the rise of the Theosophical movement but followed for ages in the East and continued down to the present day in India — that the trained man by the use of his will, mind, and imagination can disintegrate an object, send it along currents definitely existing in space, transport the mass of atoms to a distant place, passing them through certain obstacles, and reintegrate the object at the given distant spot exactly with the same visibility, limits, and appearance as it had when first taken up for transport. But this has its limitations. It cannot ordinarily be done with a human living body. That would require such an expenditure of force and so interfere with the rights of life that it may be excluded altogether. Size and resistance of obstacle have also to do with success or failure. Omnipotence of a sort that may transcend law is not admitted in Occultism; that the Adepts pointed out when they wrote that if they could at one stroke turn the world into an Arcadia for lofty souls they would do so, but the world can only be conquered step by step and under the rule of law. It is the same in all operations that copy nature either chemically or mechanically. Hence it is said in these schools that, "there are failures in occult art as well as among men". Such failures come from an inability to cope with limiting conditions. We can analyze the phenomenon of disintegration and transport of mass of matter and reintegration in this way: There is the operator who must know how to use his will, mind, and imagination. Next is the object to be dealt with. Then there is the resisting obstacle through which it may have to pass; and the air, ether, and astral light through which it travels. Lastly is the question whether or not there is the force called cohesion, by means of which masses of matter are held together within limits of form.

If it be said that the force known as gravity holds masses of matter together, we are reduced to accepting a more mysterious explanation for a common thing than the three persons in one God. But cohesion without any other postulate amounts merely to saying that masses of matter cohere because they cohere. Occultism, in common with the Vedantic philosophy, says that there is a force of cohesion, which has its roots and power in the spirit and in the ideal form; and attraction and repulsion operate from the same base also. Further, that school holds gravitation to be but an exhibition of the action of these two — attraction and repulsion. Living masses such as vegetables, animals, and men deal with matter in another state from that which is in minerals, and exhibit the quicker action of disintegrating forces; while minerals go to pieces very slowly. Both kinds are compelled in time to fall apart as masses in consequence of the action of evolutionary law when they are left altogether to themselves; that is, the whole quantity of matter of and belonging to the globe is continually subject to the hidden forces which are molding it for higher uses and turning it, however slowly, into a higher class of matter. The normal rate is what we see, but this normal rate may be altered, and that it can be altered by intelligent mind and will is the fact. This alteration of rate is seen in the forcing processes used for plants by which they are made to grow much faster than is usual under common conditions. In the same way in masses of matter which will surely go to pieces in the course of time, long or short, the molecules may be pushed apart before their time and held so by the trained will. That is, the force of repulsion can be opposed to natural attraction so as to drive the molecules apart and hold them thus away from each other. When the repulsion is slackened, the molecules rush together again to assume their former appearance. In this case the shape is not altered, but the largely diffused body of molecules retains its shape though invisible to the eye, and upon appearing to sight again it simply condenses itself into the smaller original limits, thus becoming dense enough to be once more seen and touched.

When a small object is thus disintegrated by occult means it can be passed through other objects. Or if it is to be transported without disintegration, then any dense intervening obstacle is disintegrated for a sufficient space to allow it to pass. That the latter is one of the feats of fakirs, yogis, and certain mediums can be hardly a matter of doubt except for those who deny the occult character of the cosmos. Alleged spirits in respect to this have said, "We make the intervening obstacle fluid or diffused, or do the same thing for the object transported", and for once they seem to be right. A gentleman of high character and ability in the northwest told me that one day a man unknown in his village came to the door, and exhibiting some rings of metal made one pass through the other, one of the rings seeming to melt away at the point of contact. H. P. Blavatsky has narrated to me many such cases, and I have seen her do the same thing. As, for instance, she has taken in my sight a small object such as a ring, and laying it on the table caused it to appear without her touching it inside of a closed drawer near by. Now in that instance either she disintegrated it and caused it to pass into the drawer, or disintegrated the drawer for a sufficient space, or she hypnotized me with all my senses on the alert, putting the object into the drawer while I was asleep and without my perceiving any sort of change whatever in my consciousness. The latter I cannot accept, but if it be held as true, then it was more wonderful than the other feat. The circumstances and motive were such as to exclude the hypnotizing theory; it was done to show me that such a phenomenon was possible and to give me a clue to the operation, and also to explain to me how the strange things of spiritualism might be done and, indeed, must be done under the laws of man's mind and nature.

Next we have the intelligent part of the matter to look at. Here the inner senses have to act under the guidance of a mind free from the illusions of matter, able to see into the occult cosmos behind the veil of objectivity. The will acts with immense force, exerting the powers both of attraction and repulsion as desired; knowledge of occult chemistry comes into use; the currents in the astral light or ether have to be known, as also how to make new currents. Those who have seen into the astral light and looked at the currents moving to and fro will understand this, others will either doubt, deny, or suspend judgment. The imagination as in the case of precipitation, is of prime importance; for in these things imagination is the sight and the hand of the mind and the will, without which the latter can accomplish nothing, just as the will and brain of a man whose arms are cut off can do nothing unless others aid him. But mind, will, and imagination do not reconstruct the disintegrated object, for as soon as the dispersing force is slackened from its hold on the mass of molecules, the imagination having held the image of the object, the atoms obediently and automatically rearrange themselves as before.

All this may seem fanciful, but there are those who know of their own knowledge that it is all according to fact. And it is doubtless true that in no long time modern science will begin, as it is even now slowly starting, to admit all these things by admitting in full the ideal nature of the cosmos, thus removing at once the materialistic notions of man and nature which mostly prevail at the present day.

SOME PROPOSITIONS

BY H. P. BLAVATSKY

The following is extracted from H.P.B.'s first book, and is printed in this series with the belief that it will be useful as well as interesting. She gives some fundamental oriental propositions relating to occult arts, thus:

1. There is no miracle. Everything that happens is the result of law — eternal, immutable, ever-active. Apparent miracle is but the operation of forces antagonistic to what Dr. W. B. Carpenter, F. R. S. — a man of great learning but little knowledge — calls "the well ascertained laws of nature." Like many of his class, Dr. Carpenter ignores the fact that there may be laws once "known," now unknown, to science.

2. Nature is triune: there is a visible objective nature; an invisible, indwelling, energizing nature, the exact model of the other and its vital principle; and above these two is spirit, the source of all forces, alone eternal and indestructible. The lower two constantly change; the higher third does not.

3. Man is also triune: he has his objective physical body; his vitalizing astral body (or soul), the real man; and these two are brooded over and illuminated by the third — the sovereign, the immortal spirit. When the real man succeeds in merging himself with the latter, he becomes an immortal entity.

4. *Magic, as a science, is the knowledge of these principles, and the way by which the omniscience and omnipotence of the spirit and its control over nature's forces may be acquired by the individual while still in the body. Magic, as an art, is the application of this knowledge in practice.*

5. *Arcane knowledge misapplied is sorcery; beneficently used, true magic or wisdom.*

6. *Mediumship is the opposite of Adeptship; the medium is the passive instrument of foreign influences, the Adept actively controls himself and all inferior potencies.*

7. *All things that ever were, that are, or that will be, having their record upon the astral light, or tablet of the unseen universe, the initiated Adept, by using the vision of his own spirit, can know all that has been known or can be known.*

8. *Races of men differ in spiritual gifts as in color, stature, or any other external quality; among some people seership naturally prevails, among others mediumship. Some are addicted to sorcery, and transmit its secret rules of practice from generation to generation, with a range of psychical phenomena, more or less wide, as the result.*

9. *One phase of magical skill is the voluntary and conscious withdrawal of the inner man (astral form) from the outer man (physical body). In the cases of some mediums withdrawal occurs, but it is unconscious and involuntary. With the latter the body is more or less cataleptic at such times; but with the Adept the absence of the astral form would not be noticed, for the physical senses are alert and the individual appears only as though in a fit of abstraction — "a brown study", as some call it. To the movements of the wandering astral form*

neither time nor space offers any obstacle. The thaumaturgist thoroughly skilled in occult science can cause himself (that is, his physical body) to seem to disappear or to apparently take on any shape that he may choose. He may make his astral form visible, or he may give it protean appearances. In both cases these results will be achieved by a mesmeric hallucination simultaneously brought on. This hallucination is so perfect that the subject of it would stake his life that he saw a reality, when it is but a picture in his own mind impressed upon his consciousness by the irresistible will of the mesmerizer.

But while the astral form can go anywhere, penetrate any obstacle, and be seen at any distance from the physical body, the latter is dependent upon ordinary methods of transportation. It may be levitated under prescribed magnetic conditions, but not pass from one locality to another except in the usual way. Inert matter may be in certain cases and under certain conditions disintegrated, passed through walls and recombined, but living animal organisms cannot.

Arcane science teaches that the abandonment of the living body by the soul frequently occurs, and that we encounter every day in every condition of live such living corpses. Various causes, among them overpowering fright, grief, despair, a violent attack of sickness, or excessive sensuality, may bring this about. The vacant carcass may be entered and inhabited by the astral form of an Adept, sorcerer, or an elementary (an earth-bound disembodied human soul), or, very rarely, an elemental. Of course an Adept of white magic has the same power, but unless some very exceptional and great object is to be accomplished he will never consent to pollute himself by occupying the body of an impure person. In insanity the patient's astral being is either semi-paralyzed, bewildered, and subject to the influence of every passing spirit of any sort, or it has departed forever and the body is taken possession of by some vampirish entity near its own disintegration and clinging desperately to earth whose sensual pleasures it may enjoy for a brief season longer by this expedient.

10. The corner stone of magic is an intimate practical knowledge of magnetism and electricity, their qualities, correlations, and potencies. Especially necessary is a familiarity with their effects within and upon the animal kingdom and man. There are occult properties in many other minerals equally strange with that in the loadstone, which all practitioners of magic must know and of which so-called exact science is wholly ignorant. Plants also have like mystical properties in a most wonderful degree, and the secrets of the herbs of dreams and enchantments are only lost to European science, and, useless to say too, are unknown to it except in a few marked instances such as opium and hashish. Yet the psychical effects of even these few upon the human system are regarded as evidences of a temporary mental disorder.

To sum up all in a few words; Magic is spiritual wisdom; nature the material ally, pupil, and servant of the magician. One common vital principle pervades all things, and this is controllable by the perfected human will. The Adept can stimulate the movements of the natural forces in plants and animals in a preternatural degree. Such experiments are not obstructions of nature but quickenings; the conditions of more intense vital action are given.

The Adept can control the sensations and alter the conditions of the physical and astral bodies of other persons not Adepts; he can also govern and employ as he chooses the spirits of the elements. He cannot control the immortal spirit of any human being living or dead, for all such spirits are alike sparks of the Divine Essence and not subject to any foreign domination.

Propositions 2 and 3 contain and include the seven-fold

classification. In 1877 H. P. B. was writing for those who had known but the three-fold scheme. In number two the vital principle (*prana* or *jiva*) is given; the body with vitality makes two; the real man inside called the soul, being composed of *astral body, desires*, and *mind*, makes five; the spirit, including the connecting link of *Buddhi*, completes the seven. The will is one of the forces directly from spirit, and is guided, with ordinary men, by desire; in the Adepts' case the will is guided by Buddhi, Manas, and Atma, including in its operation the force of a pure spiritual desire acting solely under law and duty.

www.ingramcontent.com/pod-product-compliance
Lightning Source LLC
LaVergne TN
LVHW041503070426
835507LV00009B/790